The American Reader

By Kathy-jo Wargin

Illustrated by K.L. Darnell

Sleeping Bear Press˙

310 North Main Street, Suite 300
Chelsea, MI 48118
www.sleepingbearpress.com

THOMSON
GALE

© 2006 Thomson Gale, a part of the Thomson Corporation.

Thomson, Star Logo and Sleeping Bear Press are trademarks
and Gale is a registered trademark used herein under license.

Printed and bound in China.

10 9 8 7 6 5 4 3 2 1

Library of Congress Cataloging-in-Publication Data

Wargin, Kathy-jo.
The American reader / by Kathy-jo Wargin ;
illustrated by K.L. Darnell.
p. cm.
Summary: "Modeled after traditional primers, this book includes individual stories and
poems about America's history, character, conservation, famous people, and national symbols"
—Provided by publisher.
ISBN 1-58536-095-3
I. United States—Literary collections. 2. United States—Juvenile literature.
I. Darnell, Kathryn, ill. II. Title.
PS3623.A74A44 2006
810.8'00—dc22   200601363

Preface

Welcome to *The American Reader*. I hope you enjoy this collection of short stories and poems and riddles about our fine country and its heritage. Long ago, small books like this were created for children to teach reading and writing skills, as well as a way to impart lessons about life and morality.

As you read along you will notice that certain poems and stories can be used as simple one-act plays or performances. You will also notice stories that teach interesting bits of our nation's history through the people and places we love. You may discover many ways to make them your own and share them with others.

In this treasury of tales you will find everything from Clara Barton to the four leaf clover, Samuel Morse and Noah Webster, our state nicknames, and American symbols to the story of our *Pledge of Allegiance*—there's something for every reader to enjoy and learn from through these short, meaningful stories.

Most of all, I hope this book inspires heartfelt conversation between young and old, creating moments and ways to share stories through the generations.

Thank you to all of the educators, librarians, and teachers who assisted me in the assembly of this book. And, thank you to the people who will read it. I hope you enjoy every bit.

Your friend,
Kathy-jo Wargin

For Jake.

KATHY-JO WARGIN

To my brother, David.

K.L. DARNELL

Table of Contents

An American Pledge
by Kathy-jo Wargin

This is our America
One land with many faces
This is our America
We come from many places

To live a life of freedom
In a land where we belong
This is our America
Forever great and strong.

North, South, East, and West

Here's to the land where cold winds blow
Here's to the land of ice and snow
Here's to the home with prairies near
Here's to the North! Home of good cheer!

Here's to the land where big cotton grows
Here's to sweet Dixie and Cherokee Rose
Here's to white blooms on magnolia trees
Here's to the South! Home of great ease!

Here's to the land where poppies unfold
Here's to the coast and hills made of gold
Here's to big redwoods and small cactus
wrens
Here's to the West! Home of kind friends!

Here's to the land where the rugged coast
   sways
Here's to the land of quaint harbors and bays
Here's to the mountains, the moose, and
   the streams
Here's to the East! Home of sweet dreams!

Ten Little Bunnies

Bunny number **one** said,
"Where can I be?"

Bunny number **two** said,
"Wait up for me!"

Bunny number **three** said,
"It's time to eat."

Bunny number **four** said,
"Tickle my feet."

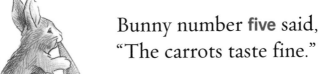

Bunny number **five** said,
"The carrots taste fine."

Bunny number **six** said,
"Those carrots are mine!"

Bunny number **seven** said,
"It's time for bed."

Bunny number **eight** said,
"Put down your head."

Bunny number **nine** said,
"Don't make a peep!"

Bunny number **ten** said,
"Baby's asleep."

Mother Bunny nodded and wiggled her ears,
and said in a whisper,

"Good night my TEN dears."

The Legend
of the Sandman

Far away, in a place with no name, lives a handsome boy with eyes of stars and a face so pale and round it is believed he is made of moondust and morning dew. Around his waist he wears a silken sash, tied and waiting with a pouch of mystery, time, and dreams. The fellow has no mother or father, no sister or brother. Yet happy is he, to live by himself in a fold of time between nighttime and morning.

Every night he peeps through keyholes
and windows locked, to spy children slip-
ping into their beds where snug beneath
their blankets they drift along the border
of wake and sleep.

In his dream-cap he walks, gliding into
each room like a cloud itself, so light on his
feet that it seems he can fly. With a smile
full of dreams and a wink of his star-eyes
he dances around, tossing tiny grains from
his pouch, landing here and there about
each bed, until all children fall into the
deep sleep where dreams are possible.

It is not until morning, when children wake to find tiny specks of sleep dust beneath their eyes, that they know of his visit. For these tiny bits of moon and stars and clouds and magic could only come from him, their dream-fellow friend, the Sandman.

A Nonsense Poem

Goober Topsy
Fabber Popsy
Bumble Frumpy
Baby Mopsy

Tilly woober
Dilly floober
Happy Sneeker
Billy Goopy

Oh my! Let's all try.

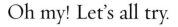

Bedder Lumpy
Tipper Rumpy
Flopsy doodle
Noodle grumpy

Wipper noggen
Looper doggen
Silly Booty
Foober Woggen

Oh no, way too slow,
one more time,
get set and go!

vocabulary: journey / coyotes / forests
Everglades / tide pools / heartland

The Moon and Stars
Above America

Let us play a game. Night has fallen upon our country, and we are the moon and the stars floating high above the land. What do we see?

Moon: I see the lazy Mississippi River sway from side to side as it makes its way from the north to the south. It begins its journey as a small brook in Minnesota, bubbling over rocks and grasses, and grows wider and faster as it makes its way to the Gulf of Mexico.

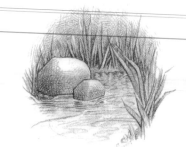

Stars: We see coyotes dashing through western deserts, kicking up dust and playing in the night near the Grand Canyon. We hear them howl in the moonlight, looking to the sky as they yip and sing.

Moon: I see dark and deep forests of the north where deer and moose bed down for the night. I see mother bears leading their cubs down narrow pathways, teaching them secrets about life in the woods.

Stars: We see thick damp mosses of the Florida Everglades hanging above still waters. There are birds and turtles tucked into its grassy banks, while fish swim nearby, making soft ripples in the moonlight.

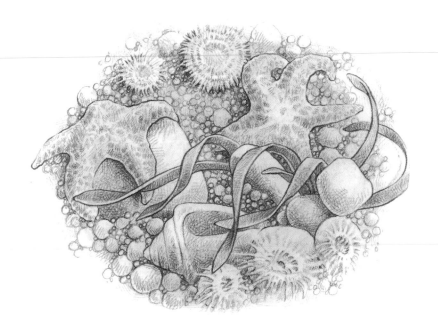

Moon: I see ocean tide pools fill with starfish and seashells and weeds, treasures from the ocean that wait to be found in the morning. Out in the distance, whales and dolphins leap out of the water as if they are dancing for joy.

Stars: We see bright lights and fast cars race through the city of New York. We see people dressed in colorful clothes, walking up and down the streets while music pours from the theaters on Broadway.

Moon: I see the rolling fields of the heartland growing in the night, while earth brings forth new stands of corn and wheat and oats. I see farmers getting ready for a new day, lacing their boots and putting on their caps.

Stars: We see sweet young children tucked in bed, dreaming of tomorrow, sound asleep while the world outside waits.

Good night dear Moon.
Good night dear Stars.
Good night dear children.
Good night America.

One Dream at a Time

How does a spider spin a web?
One strand at a time.

How does a king make a castle?
One stone at a time.

How does a bird build a nest?
One twig at a time.

How do you walk a mile?
One footstep at a time.

How do you grow a forest?
One tree at a time.

22

How do you plant a garden?
One seed at a time.

How does a sparrow sing its song?
One note at a time.

How do you make a new friend?
One smile at a time.

How do you change the world?
One kind deed at a time.

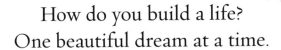

How do you build a life?
One beautiful dream at a time.

Our Symbols

One day came a lady from France,
to stand in a harbor of chance
for people to see
that her country is free
in the arms of her strong willing stance.

The Statue of Liberty in New York City harbor is 151 feet tall, and a symbol of freedom throughout the world. Made of copper, her right hand holds a burning torch, meant to represent liberty. In her left hand is a tablet with the date of July 4, 1776 inscribed in Roman numerals, which is the day the United States declared independence from England. The seven rays upon her crown symbolize the seven seas and continents, and her formal name is *Liberty Enlightening the World*.

"Give me your tired, your poor,
Your huddled masses yearning to breathe free,
The wretched refuse of your teeming shore.
Send these, the homeless, tempest-tossed to me.
I lift my lamp beside the golden door."

A bell came from London so dear
and rings so that people will hear
a declaration once signed
by a Congress so kind
is our reason to ring every year.

The Liberty Bell rang out when the Declaration of Independence was signed by the Continental Congress. Cast in London, England in 1752 and brought to America, it was originally made for the Pennsylvania State House to celebrate the 50 year anniversary of the 1701 Charter of Privileges. Shortly after the bell arrived in Philadelphia it cracked, and has been recast three times. Today there remains a thin crack in the bell, which is housed in the Liberty Bell Pavilion in Philadelphia. Yet even so, it rings every July 4th to remind us of our liberty and freedom.

How George Washington did love the rose
a treat for the eyes and the nose
later the power
a national flower
the Rose Garden happily grows.

The rose is the national floral emblem of the United States of America. It is believed to be more than 30 million years old, and has served as a symbol of love and war throughout the world. In 1986 President Ronald Reagan signed a resolution to make the rose our official emblem. George Washington, our first president, was fond of roses, and liked to grow them.

Along came a wave in the night
red for valor and pureness in white
blue justice all told
stars of heaven unfold
thirteen stripes spreading rays of the light.

The first Flag Act was passed on June 14, 1777 by the Continental Congress and stated: "Resolved, That the flag of the United States be made of thirteen stripes, alternate red and white; that the union be thirteen stars, white in a blue field, representing a new Constellation." When the Great Seal of 1782 was prepared, the colors were given their own meanings: red for valor and bravery; white for purity and innocence; and blue for vigilance, perseverance, and justice. Along the way, we added more stars as more states joined the union. Today we have 50 stars on our flag.

Frontiers held a bird marked with white
a majestic and beautiful sight
with symbolic delay
turkeys got in the way
now our freedom takes wing on its flight.

The bald eagle is not bald, it is simply marked with a white head when mature. The bald eagle became the national bird of the United States of America in 1782. But it wasn't without many years of debate in Congress. At one time the wild turkey was said to be a candidate for the symbol. But in the end it was realized that the bald eagle represented courage, strength, and freedom, and would be a much better-looking symbol for our country. Today we see the bald eagle as a symbol in many ways, such as upon the one dollar bill, the Great Seal, and the President's Flag.

Clara Barton

Clara Barton was living in Washington, D.C. during the time of a battle called First Bull Run, and learned that many of the soldiers had suffered not only from their wounds, but from not having medical supplies. Wanting to help, she advertised for donations to help the soldiers, and when she received the supplies, went to work distributing them among the needy. This was successful, and the next year the U.S. Surgeon General gave Clara Barton a pass to ride along in the army ambulances with the purpose of giving care and comfort to the sick and wounded.

For the next three years Clara Barton
followed the campaign through Virginia
and Charleston, South Carolina, where
she nursed hundreds during the Battle of
the Wilderness. Her caring ways attracted
much attention throughout the nation,
and provided much of the framework for
an organization she founded in 1881 to
help those in need. This organization was
called the American Red Cross.

Story of the Pledge of Allegiance

The first pledge to our flag was given through the National Public School Celebration of Columbus Day in 1892. It was written by Mr. Francis Bellamy for a publication called the *Youth's Companion*. The pledge was given to all public schools for children to recite in the hope they would become patriotic citizens.

That first pledge said this:

I pledge allegiance to my Flag, and to the Republic for which it stands, one nation indivisible, with liberty and justice for all.

35

In 1923 we added the words *United States* so that newcomers from other countries would know that the pledge they were saying was for the United States flag.

*I pledge allegiance to the Flag of the **United States**, and to the Republic for which it stands, one nation indivisible, with liberty and justice for all.*

In 1924 we added the words *of America*.

*I pledge allegiance to the Flag of the United States **of America**, and to the Republic for which it stands, one nation indivisible, with liberty and justice for all.*

In 1954 we added the words **under God**.
Our pledge now reads:

> *I pledge allegiance to the Flag of the United*
> *States of America, and to the Republic for*
> *which it stands, one nation **under God***
> *indivisible, with liberty and justice for all.*

In 1942 it became the official pledge of
the United States, but was still called
The Pledge to the Flag. In 1945 it received
its official title, *The Pledge of Allegiance.*

State Nicknames

Do you have a nickname? Sometimes a nickname describes something we like about ourselves. States have nicknames too! If you could give yourself a nickname, what would it be?

Alabama: the Yellowhammer State

Alaska: The Last Frontier

Arizona: The Grand Canyon State

Arkansas : The Natural State

California: The Golden State

Colorado: The Centennial State

Connecticut: Constitution State

Delaware: The First State

Florida: The Sunshine State

Georgia: The Peach State

Hawaii: The Aloha State

Idaho: The Gem State

Illinois: The Prairie State

Indiana: Hoosier State

Iowa: Hawkeye State

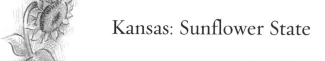

Kansas: Sunflower State

Kentucky: Bluegrass State

Louisiana: Pelican State

Maine: Pine Tree State

Maryland: Old Line State

Massachusetts: Bay State

Michigan: Wolverine State

Minnesota: North Star State

Mississippi: Magnolia State

Missouri: Show Me State

Montana: Treasure State

 Nebraska: Cornhusker State

Nevada: The Silver State

New Hampshire:
The Granite State

New Jersey: Garden State

New Mexico:
Land of Enchantment

New York: Empire State

North Carolina: Tar Heel State

North Dakota: Peace Garden State

Ohio: Buckeye State

Oklahoma: Sooner State

 Oregon: Beaver State

Pennsylvania: Keystone State

Rhode Island:
The Ocean State

South Carolina: Palmetto State

South Dakota: Mount Rushmore State

Tennessee: The Volunteer State

Texas: Lone Star State

Utah: The Beehive State

Vermont: Green Mountain State

Virginia: Old Dominion State

Washington:
The Evergreen State

West Virginia: The Mountain State

Wisconsin: The Badger State

Wyoming: Equality State

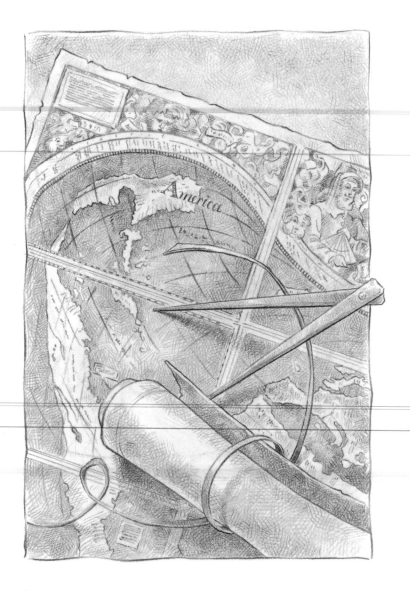

Amerigo

Amerigo Vespucci was born in Florence, Italy in 1454. As a young man, he liked books and maps, and studied under a famous painter named Michelangelo. In 1492, while working for bankers, Amerigo was sent to Spain. He liked it there very much and seven years later, while still in Spain, was sent on an expedition to explore the coast of what would someday be known as South America.

Amerigo spent the next several years exploring and recording his travels. He kept journals of his experiences. In 1508 he was named the Pilot Major of Spain, which was a great honor.

During one of his expeditions, Amerigo Vespucci realized that he wasn't looking at India, as thought by Columbus who had been there shortly before him, but a new place on a newly discovered continent. Although Columbus had been there first while seeking a passage to the east, it was Amerigo Vespucci who realized this land was indeed a new continent.

The diaries and journals of Amerigo Vespucci and his travels became very popular in Florence, Italy. A mapmaker named Waldseemüller read the entries and believed that Amerigo was responsible for the discovery of this new world. When Waldseemüller created a woodblock map

of Amerigo's travels, he printed the name "America" on the land that Amerigo realized was a new continent. America is a version of his name, Amerigo.

These maps were published widely, and in time, many people began to know these new continents as North and South America.

Later, based on disagreement about who actually "discovered" this land, Waldseemüller thought perhaps he should change the name on the map he printed. But it was too late! The name America had been accepted. Today, we know our country as the United States of America.

I Am a Citizen of the United States of America

I belong to a country that allows me to live a free life, to be who I want to be, and to say what I want to say.

Liberty

I have the right to liberty. This means I can be who I want to be. I can vote for the people I believe in, and express my opinion to my government.

Pursuit of Happiness

I have the right to pursue a happy life. I am allowed to do what I enjoy as long as I do not hurt others in the process.

Common Good

I will work for the common good, which means I will do my share to help my community and shape the world we live in.

Justice

I will treat people fairly. This means that no people or groups of people will be favored over another.

Equality

All people are equal. This means all people have a right to the same treatment regardless of the color of their skin, whether they are a boy or girl, what their religious beliefs are, where they come from, who their ancestors are, or if they are rich or poor.

Diversity

I will appreciate the differences in our culture such as the way we dress, our heritage, and the language we speak. We are all special.

Truth

I will expect the government to be truthful at all times. This means that I have the right to be told truthful information at all times by all people of the government.

Patriotism

I can use words or actions to declare my love for my country.

Popular Sovereignty

Our government belongs to the people, and gets its power from the people. I am one of the people, and we have authority over the government.

The Four Leaf Clover

I know a place where the clover grows
In lovely rows
Beneath my toes

Down in the meadow a gentle brook
and grassy nook
For me to look

I'll find a clover — four leaves on
Deep in a lawn
I lay upon

One leaf for hope
The world be kind
One leaf for faith
To see when blind

One leaf for love
That hearts may bind
One leaf for luck
All four we find

I know a place where the clover grows
In lovely rows
Beneath my toes

Down in the meadow a gentle brook
and grassy nook
For me to look

I found a clover — four leaves on
and what fine luck
for me to pluck!

Dits and Dahs – The Morse Code

Tiny dots and dashes make words for us to read.
But how can that be? What do they mean?

Samuel Finley Breese Morse was an inventor. In the 1830s he invented an electric telegraph, which is a small machine that relays a series of electric signals over wires. This was the first electric device to send messages. It works by tapping out a code for each alphabet letter of the message using a telegraph key. Short signals are called dits and long signals are called dahs. When it is written out on a piece of paper, a dit would be shown as a dot, and a dah would be shown as a dash.

This way of sending messages by a series of dits and dahs became known as Morse Code. When using Morse Code, it is important to know the correct amount of time to wait between letters and words. A dit is one unit of time, a dah is three units of time. A pause between letters is three units of time, and a pause between sentences is seven units of time. By the 1850s, Morse Code was used throughout the world. One of the most well-known Morse Code messages is this: ··· — — — ···

Do you know what this means?

It is well known throughout the world that ··· — — — ··· means SOS.

Here is the Morse Code Alphabet. Can you send a message to your friends?

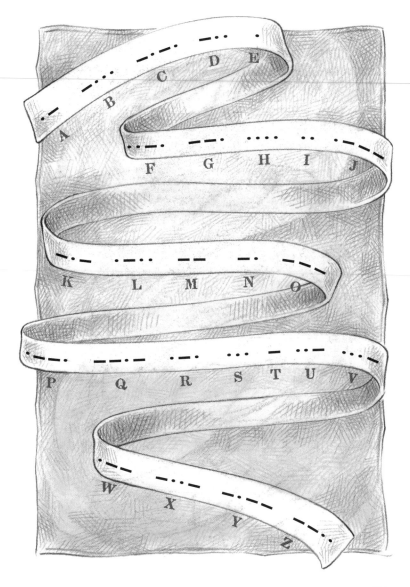

The Star-Spangled Banner

The war of 1812 was between the United States of America and the British. During that time, a young Washington attorney named Francis Scott Key discovered that the British Army was holding his friend, Dr. William Beanes, as a prisoner. In an attempt to save his friend, he and an American Agent for Prisoner Exchange sailed out to Chesapeake Bay to meet with the British Royal Navy. The British agreed to release Dr. Beanes, but made the three wait under guard until the British had attacked Fort McHenry, an American fort built to defend Baltimore, Maryland.

The trio was forced to watch the bombing of the American fort. Through the smoke and haze, Francis Scott Key could see that our United States flag was still waving, and this gave him hope. On a piece of paper he had in his pocket, he wrote a poem he called the "Defense of Fort McHenry." Later, that poem became known as *The Star-Spangled Banner* and in 1931 became the United States National Anthem.

Oh, say can you see, by the dawn's
early light,
What so proudly we hailed at the twilight's
last gleaming?
Whose broad stripes and bright stars,
through the perilous fight,
O'er the ramparts we watched, were so
gallantly streaming?
And the rockets' red glare, the bombs
bursting in air,
Gave proof through the night that our
flag was still there.
O say, does that star-spangled banner
yet wave
O'er the land of the free and the home
of the brave?

The Story of Hotfoot Teddy

CHAPTER ONE

A Little Cub

A long time ago in New Mexico, a bear cub ran through the meadows of Lincoln National Forest. The bear played all day long, rolling in the grass and warming himself beneath the sun. But as the little cub played, somewhere in the forest a spark burst into a flame.

That flame grew into more flames, and suddenly the forest was ablaze. The trees began to catch fire and the grasses burned quickly. All of the animals began to run for safety. And so did the little bear cub.

CHAPTER TWO
The Forest Fire

The little cub felt scared. He had never seen a forest fire before, and it was hot and noisy. He saw firefighters struggle in the forest, trying to tame wild flames as they cracked and whipped through the trees. The little cub was so frightened he climbed a burned tree and waited there for his mother. But he could not see his mother. He could not see his friends. His forest was not a forest anymore. It was an empty place with black tree trunks sticking out from every direction. There were clouds and rings of dull gray smoke hanging in the air. The little bear cub stayed in the tree and waited.

CHAPTER THREE
A Little Cub Saved

When the firefighters finished putting out the fire, they saw the cub in the tree. He looked scared and hungry, so they took him down and brought him to a safe place and gave him the nickname "Hotfoot Teddy."

The little cub had burned paws and legs. The game warden put the bear in an airplane and brought him to a doctor in Santa Fe. The animal doctor took good care of the cub, and the warden and his family helped, too. Because he was injured in a forest fire they renamed him Smokey, and decided that he should be the symbol for a public service campaign that started years before.

CHAPTER FOUR

A New Home for Smokey

But Smokey no longer had a home. His home had been destroyed by fire. So the people who helped Smokey decided to put him on an airplane and send him to the National Zoo in Washington, D.C.

Smokey grew up into a very fine bear. Boys and girls from across the country came to see him, and learned how to prevent forest fires. The little cub soon became known as the living symbol for fire prevention. He died in 1976 and is buried at the Smokey Bear Historical Park in New Mexico.

Tips to Prevent Forest Fires

- Never leave a fire burning if you are not around to watch it.
- Always have a shovel and water nearby.
- Make sure your fire is out before you leave the area.
- Make sure there are no branches or dry sticks hanging above your fire.
- Never take burning sticks out of a fire.
- Never use fireworks on public land.
- If you see a fire, contact the Ranger as soon as possible.

Noah Webster

A Colonial Boy

Long ago during the time of George Washington, there lived a young boy named Noah Webster. Noah lived in Connecticut where his father was a farmer and a weaver. His family lived a good colonial life.

Noah loved books. Noah loved school. In 1774 when he was sixteen years old, he set out for Yale, Connecticut's only college at the time. This was during the Revolutionary War, and times soon became hard for everyone. Noah loved learning so much that he wanted to stay in college and attend law school. But Noah couldn't afford to attend, so he went to work as a teacher.

The Blue-backed Speller

Noah liked being a teacher. He worked in a one-room schoolhouse with many children, and he loved to help them learn new things. But he did not like some of the textbooks that the children had to use. Many of those textbooks were from England, and Noah thought American children should have American schoolbooks. So Noah Webster decided to write his own schoolbooks for children.

It did not take long before one of his first books became very popular. It was called the *Elementary Spelling Book.* This book had a blue cover, so over time it became known as the "blue-backed speller."

Many people learned to read and spell from a blue-backed speller, and this made Noah very successful. But there was one more thing Noah Webster wanted to do.

An American Hero

During this time, America was filled with people who had come from other places. They spoke different languages, spelled words differently, and did not pronounce words the same way. Noah Webster thought that because America was now its own country, all Americans should speak and spell the same way.

So he decided to write a book to help people do this. It took him more than 27 years to finish it, but when he did, he became an American hero. This book had more than 70,000 words in it, and was called *An American Dictionary of the English Language*. Later, it became known as the *Merriam-Webster Dictionary*.

vocabulary: apartment / wheelchair
accident / etiquette / assist

Jack's Neighbor

Jack and his mother live in a city. They live on a busy street where rows of apartment houses stand like towers above long, straight sidewalks.

It was a sunny morning, so they walked to the grocery store. Jack and his mother enjoyed looking at the colorful flowers set in pots upon front porches, and waving hello to neighbors as they passed by. Soon, Jack and his mother were walking in front of Mr. Paulson's apartment.

Jack's hands and face felt like they were getting warm when they walked past Mr. Paulson's apartment. Please, he thought to himself, please let's just keep walking by.

But Jack's mother stopped.

"Jack," she said, "let's go in and ask Mr. Paulson if he needs anything from the grocery store."

Jack looked down at his feet and said, "I think we should just keep walking, Mom. I am sure he doesn't need anything from the store."

Jack's mother knew right away that something was wrong. Mr. Paulson used a wheelchair, and she and Jack never really spoke about it.

"Jack," she said, "are you afraid of
Mr. Paulson?"

"Yes, no, sort of" Jack replied.

"But why?" asked his mother.

"I don't know, I just don't know what to say to him. Does he feel bad about using a wheelchair? Will he ever get out? How did he get into it?"

"Jack," said his mother, "Mr. Paulson is a person with a disability. He was in a car accident many years ago. The accident hurt his legs and now they don't work. I am sure that Mr. Paulson did feel bad at first, but he doesn't anymore. The wheelchair helps him do most things he used to do."

"But then why do we need to ask if he needs anything from the store?" replied Jack. "Won't he feel bad if you ask him that?" "Jack," said his mother with a warm smile, "Mr. Paulson has a bad cold, and I would offer to get groceries for any neighbor who has bad cold."

With that, Jack smiled at his mother. They walked hand in hand up Mr. Paulson's sidewalk and rang the doorbell together.

Etiquette

A disability simply means that a person may need to do things differently.

1. Good etiquette means shaking hands when you meet or see a person. If the person cannot shake hands with his right hand, use the left. If the person cannot shake hands at all, you can nod, smile, or touch that person on the shoulder or arm to let him know that you are saying hello.

2. Never lean on a person's wheelchair. His wheelchair is his personal space and property.

3. When you are talking to a person in a wheelchair who has a helper along, look and speak directly to the person in the wheelchair—not the helper.

4. Offer assistance with warmth and respect. Do not proceed to assist someone who has politely told you "No thank you."

5. If someone says yes, he would like some help, listen carefully to his instructions.

6. If someone can't see well, let him hold onto your arm near your elbow.

7. Offer to help in a warm way, such as "May I help you with your packages?"

8. If you want to ask someone about his or her disability, ask in a polite and respectful manner.

Art in the Park

In the early 1800s America was growing very fast. Colonists and settlers in the east heard about great amounts of gold being found in the west, and they wanted to try their luck at finding some for themselves. As these newcomers began to move across the United States, they began to see how beautiful our country really was.

George Catlin was an artist who created paintings about life on this vast frontier. He also liked to paint pictures of Native Americans and the true way in which they lived. He loved the wild frontier and all its beauty. But George Catlin grew worried that all these new settlers might have a bad effect on the native populations, the wilderness, and the wildlife that lived there.

George Catlin wanted to make a difference. He used his paintings to show people the beauty of the west, and to make them aware of how special it was. In 1832 he wrote a statement that said the elements of our wilderness should be preserved "by some great protecting policy of government... in a magnificent park... A nation's park, containing man and beast, in all the wild freshness of their nature's beauty!"

At that time, not all people thought about the wilderness the same way that George Catlin did. Many people thought the wilderness was better used for mining and farming and building towns. But even so, George Catlin never gave up.

Years later, in 1864, Congress donated Yosemite Valley to California for preservation as a state park. In 1872, Congress set aside the Yellowstone area in the Wyoming and Montana territories "as a public park or pleasuring-ground for the benefit and enjoyment of the people."

But at that time, there was no organization to oversee Yellowstone, so it remained in the custody of the U.S. Department of the Interior, where it became our first national park. Congress would then proceed to create more national parks, which we enjoy today.

Some of the National Parks
that may sound familiar to you are:

Acadia National Park, *Maine*
Everglades National Park, *Florida*
Glacier National Park, *Montana*
Denali National Park and Preserve, *Alaska*
Great Smoky Mountains National Park,
North Carolina and Tennessee
Zion National Park, *Utah*
Badlands National Park, *South Dakota*
Grand Canyon National Park, *Arizona*
Big Bend National Park, *Texas*
Voyageurs National Park, *Minnesota*

Kathy-jo Wargin

Author Kathy-jo Wargin has written more than 20 books for children, including such award-winning titles as IRA Teachers' Choices Award *Win One for the Gipper*; Midwest Booksellers Favorite *The Legend of the Lady's Slipper*; and Children's Choice Award Winner *The Legend of the Loon*. She has also written *B is for Badger: A Wisconsin Alphabet*; the newly-released *A Mother's Wish*; and Michigan Notable Book Award Winner *The Edmund Fitzgerald: Song of the Bell*. Kathy-jo is also the author of *The Michigan Reader for Boys and Girls*.

Ms. Wargin travels frequently to speak to schoolchildren around the country, sharing ideas about the creative process, helping them find their creative spirit, and what it's like to be an author. Born and raised in northern Minnesota, Kathy-jo Wargin makes her home in Petoskey, Michigan.

K.L. Darnell

Artist Kate Darnell has been drawing for as long as she can remember. She earned her BFA studying drawing and painting at the University of Michigan School of Art and Design. *The American Reader* is Ms. Darnell's sixth children's book with Sleeping Bear Press. She also illustrated *The Michigan Reader for Boys and Girls*, *Fibblestax*, *Hannah and the Homunculus*, *Treasures of the Heart*, and *My Piggy Bank*. In addition to her work as an illustrator, Kate specializes in the beautiful art of calligraphy and is an instructor of art at Lansing Community College. She lives in East Lansing with her husband and daughter.